Ana Cláudia Rodovalho • Karina Torres F. Silva • Luciana Renda B. Melo

Spaghetti Kids

EDIÇÃO ATUALIZADA

2º ANO

Student's Book

MACMILLAN

Table of Contents

INTRODUCTION

CHARACTER PRESENTATION

Unit 1 • Lesson 1

WHAT'S YOUR NAME?

1. LOOK, LISTEN AND POINT.

2. ASK YOUR FRIENDS AND COMPLETE.

1. TIAGO
2. ______
3. ______
4. ______
5. ______
6. ______

3. WRITE THE NAMES.

SUZANA

______

______

______

Unit 1 • Lesson 2

1. LISTEN AND SAY.

2. SAY HELLO TO YOUR FRIENDS.

3. LET´S SING!

THE HELLO SONG

EVERYBODY SAY HELLO,

SAY HELLO, SAY HELLO.

EVERYBODY SAY HELLO.

HELLO,

4. LISTEN AND ANSWER.

	YES	NO
1. 		
2. 		
3. 		

	YES	NO
4. 		
5. 		
6. 		

Unit 1 • Lesson 3

1. LISTEN AND SAY.

2. FIND OUT THE WORDS AND MATCH.

GOOD MRNIONG

GDOO NHGIT

DOOG ANOOTFERN

GOBODEY

3. COMPLETE AND COLOR.

1. LISTEN AND CIRCLE.

1.   

2.   

3.   

4.   

2. COMPLETE

VALUES
BE POLITE

I'M FINE. HELLO! HOW ARE YOU? HI.

3. LOOK AND STICK.

LOOK!

4. LISTEN AND SAY.

READ

LISTEN

5. READ AND STICK.

LISTEN

READ

Unit 1

1. UNSCRAMBLE THE NAMES, MATCH AND COLOR.

SAUZNA

SUZANA

NEJIK

ALUOP

NAN

RCINSCFAO

ANAIULC

2. LOOK AND COMPLETE WITH THE SENTENCES FROM THE BOXES.

GOOD NIGHT.

I'M FINE.

MY NAME IS ANN.

GOOD MORNING.

MY SCHOOL OBJECTS

1. LOOK, LISTEN AND SAY.

2. MATCH

BOOK

RULER

SCHOOLBAG

PENCIL CASE

PENCIL

Unit 2 • Lesson 6

1. LET´S SING!

I SEE A PENCIL

A PENCIL, A PENCIL,

A PENCIL, I SEE.

A PENCIL, A PENCIL.

JUST FOR ME!

DO YOU, DO YOU, DO YOU SEE? (2X)

A PENCIL JUST FOR ME?

BOOK

CRAYON

2. JOIN THE DOTS, COLOR AND SAY THE WORDS.

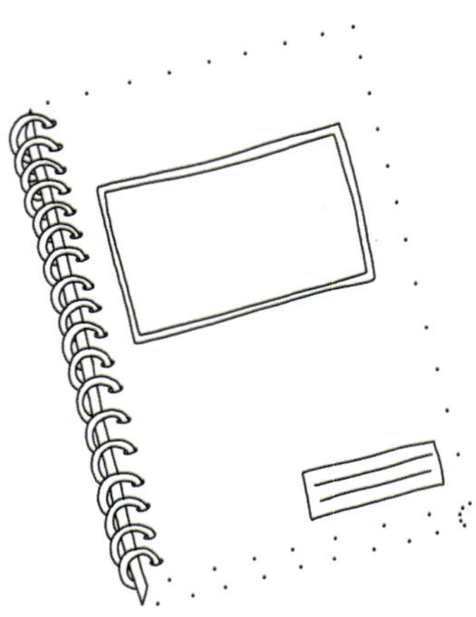

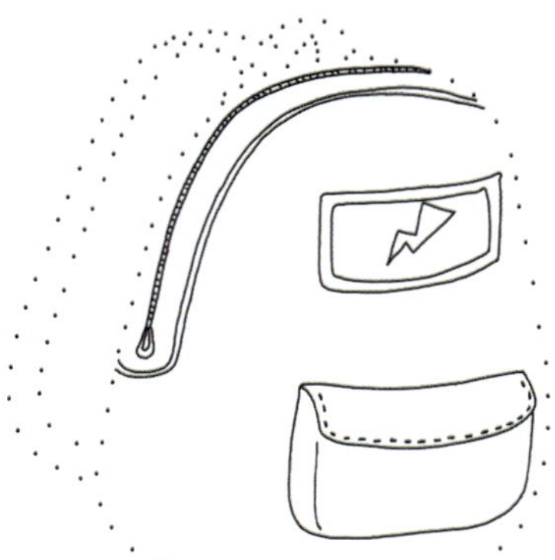

3. FIND THE WORDS.

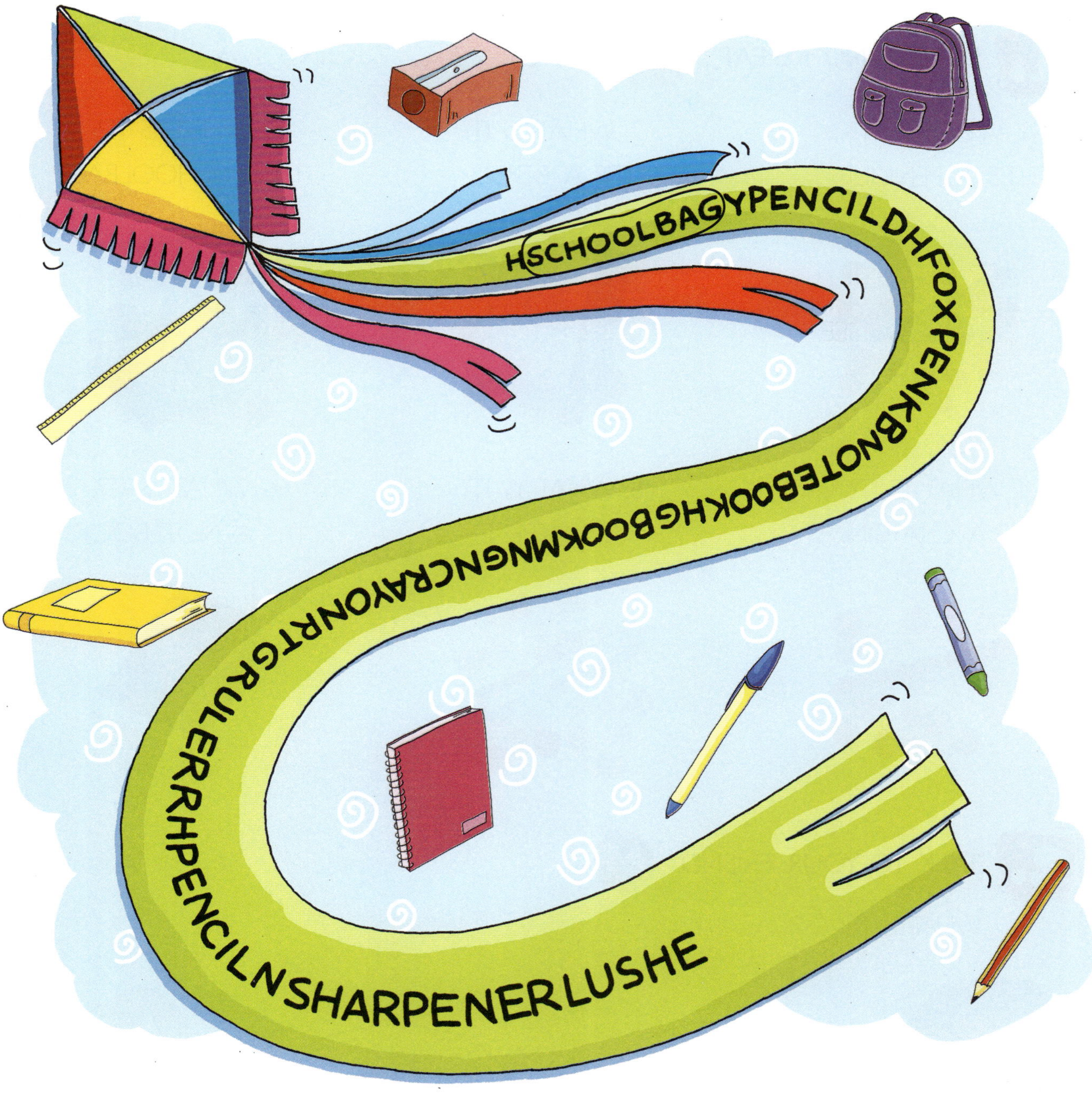

4. COMPLETE THE WORDS.

SC ___ OOLB ___ G

N ___ TE ___ OOK

PEN ___ IL

C ___ AYON

___ EN

B ___ OK

Unit 2 • Lesson 7

1. LISTEN AND REPEAT.

1. WHAT IS IT?
IT'S A PENCIL.

2. WHAT IS IT?
IT'S A BOOK.

3. WHAT IS IT?
IT'S A SCHOOLBAG.

4. WHAT IS IT?
IT'S A CRAYON.

5. WHAT IS IT?
IT'S A PEN.

6. WHAT IS IT?
IT'S A NOTEBOOK.

2. TALK TO YOUR FRIEND.

WHAT IS IT?

3. FOLLOW THE LINES AND STICK.

IT'S A BOOK.

IT'S A CRAYON.

IT'S A PENCIL CASE.

IT'S A PEN.

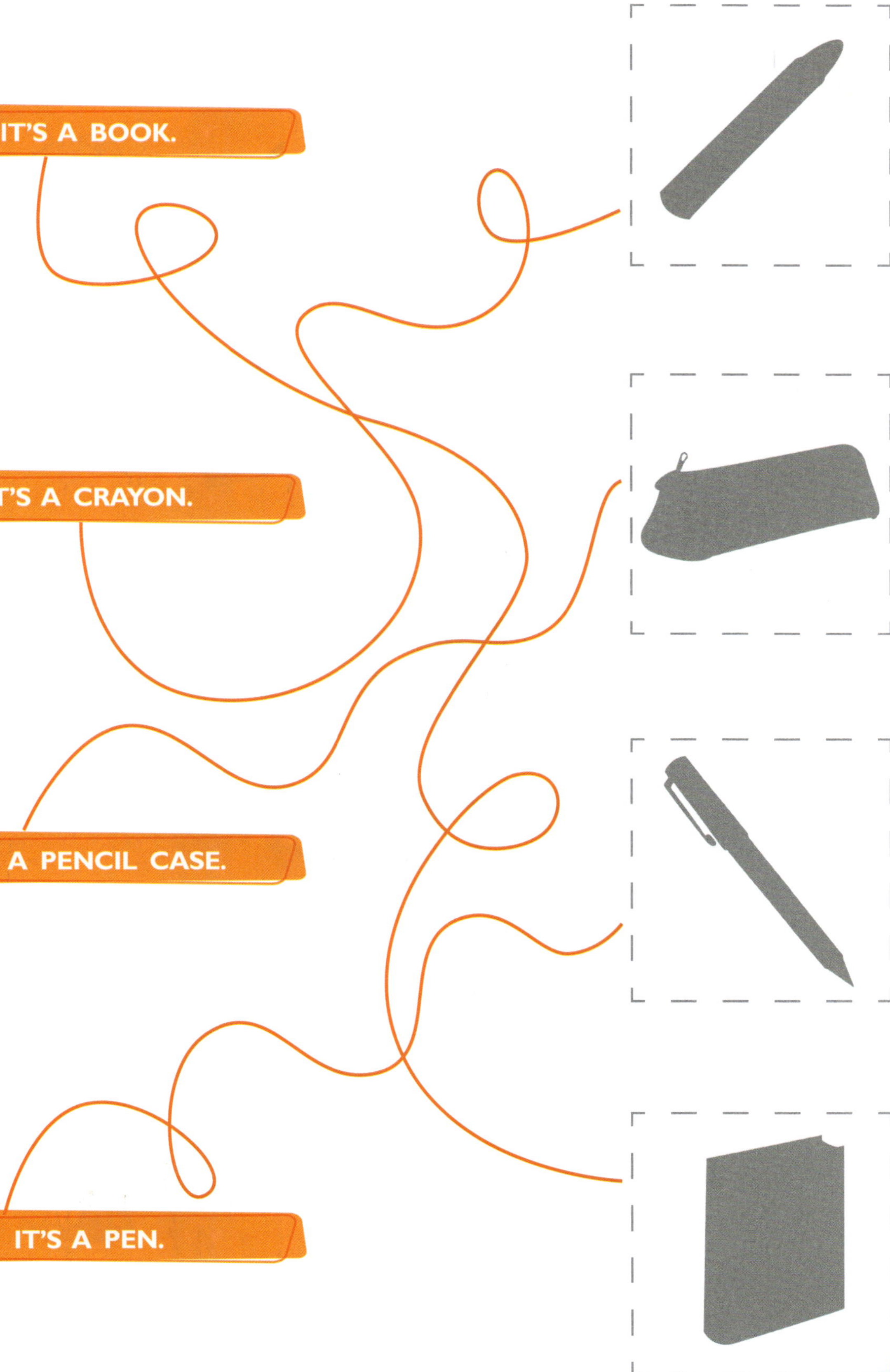

Unit 2 • Lesson 8

1. LISTEN AND CIRCLE.

1. 

2. 

3. 

4. 

5. 

6. 

LOOK!

2. COMPLETE

__ __ __ __ YOUR BOOK.

__ __ __ __ __ YOUR BOOK.

OPEN - CLOSE

3. BOARD GAME

Start
1
WHAT IS IT?
IT'S A
2
WHAT'S YOUR NAME?
3
WHAT IS IT?
IT'S A
4
WHAT IS IT?
IT'S A
5
MISS A TURN.
6
YOUR BOOK.
7
YOUR BOOK.
8
TAKE ANOTHER TURN.
9
WHAT IS IT?
IT'S A
10
WHAT IS IT?
IT'S A
11
GO TO START.
12
MISS A TURN.
13
WHAT IS IT?
IT'S A
14
WHAT IS IT?
IT'S A
Finish

EXTRA WORK

Unit 2

1. DRAW THE OBJECTS IN THE SCHOOLBAG.

- A BOOK
- A PENCIL
- A NOTEBOOK
- A PEN
- CRAYONS
- A RULER
- A PENCIL CASE

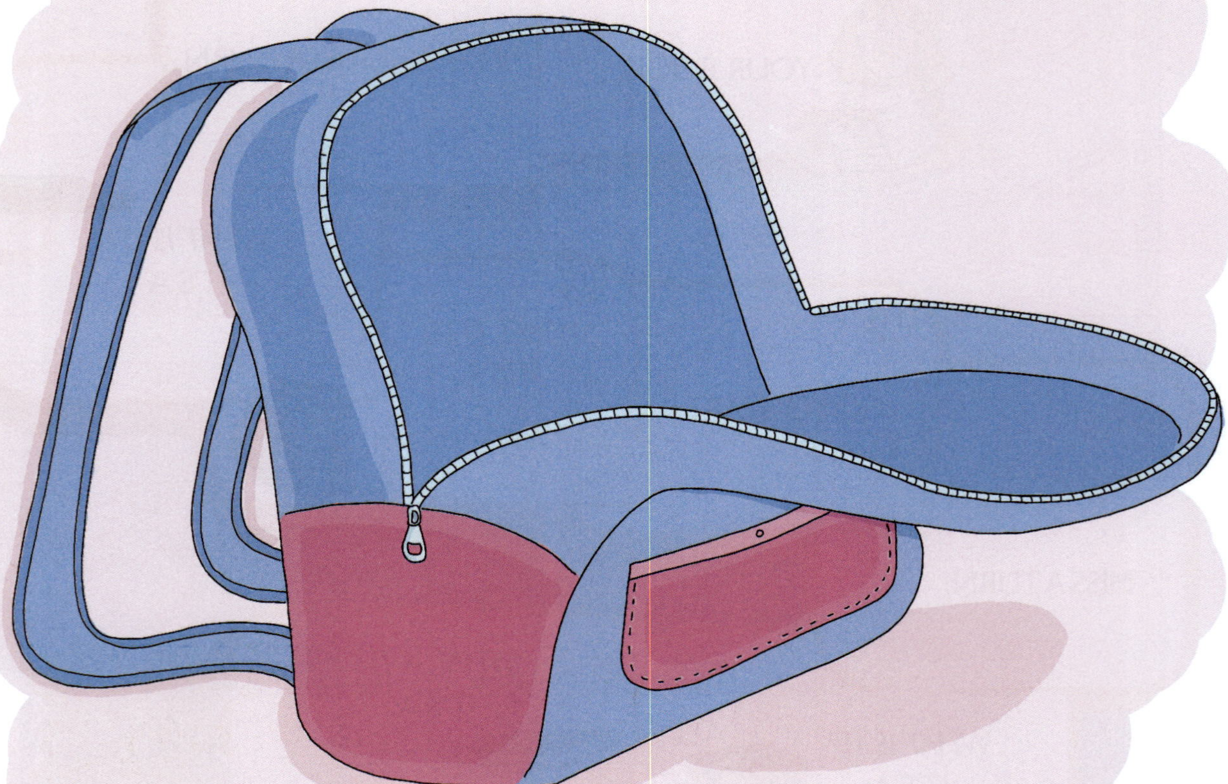

2. FIND AND COLOR SIX SCHOOL OBJECTS.

Unit 3 • Lesson 9

WHAT COLOR IS IT?

1. LOOK, LISTEN AND SAY.

2. STICK

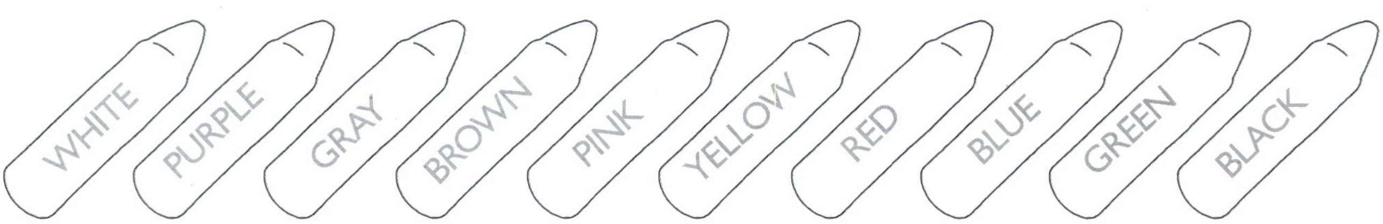

3. HELP ANN.

CUT AND GLUE.

Unit 3 • Lesson 10

1. LOOK AT THE CODE AND COLOR.

1. BLUE
2. RED
3. GREEN
4. YELLOW
5. BLACK
6. PINK
7. PURPLE
8. BROWN
9. GRAY

2. YES OR NO?

1. THE 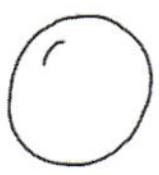 IS RED.
2. THE  IS PINK.
3. THE  IS BLACK.
4. THE  IS YELLOW.
5. THE  IS BLUE.

YES	NO

3. LISTEN AND CIRCLE. 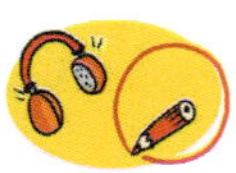

1. 
2. 
3. 
4. 
5. 
6. 

Unit 3 • Lesson 11

1. LOOK AND MATCH.

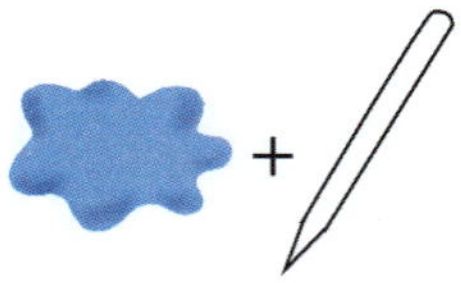

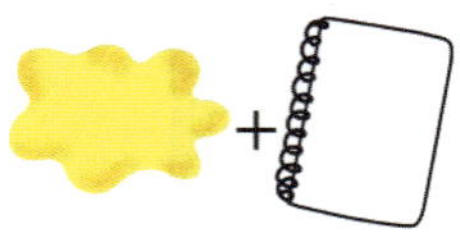

IT'S A PINK SCHOOLBAG.

IT'S A GREEN BOOK.

IT'S A PURPLE PEN.

IT'S A BLACK CRAYON.

IT'S A YELLOW NOTEBOOK.

IT'S A BLUE PENCIL.

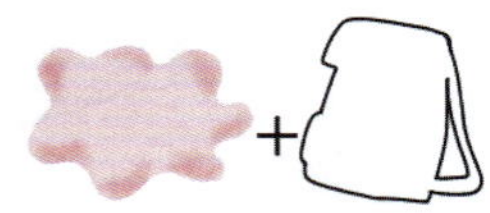

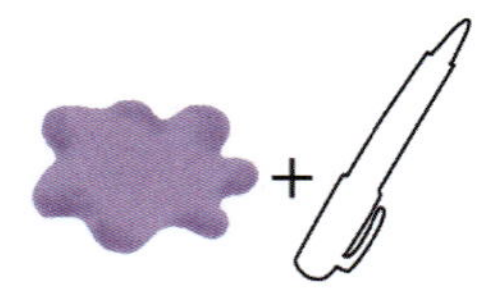

2. LISTEN AND CHECK. WHAT COLOR IS IT?

1.  ☐ GRAY ☐ YELLOW ☐ GREEN
2.  ☐ WHITE ☐ PINK ☐ BROWN
3.  ☐ PURPLE ☐ RED ☐ BLACK
4. 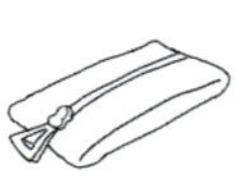 ☐ BLUE ☐ PURPLE ☐ YELLOW
5. 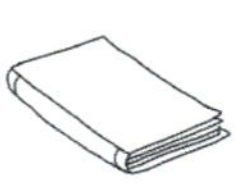 ☐ GREEN ☐ BLACK ☐ WHITE
6.  ☐ BROWN ☐ WHITE ☐ PURPLE

3. LET'S PLAY BINGO. CUT AND PLAY.

	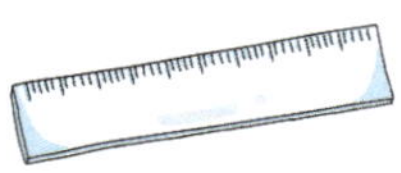	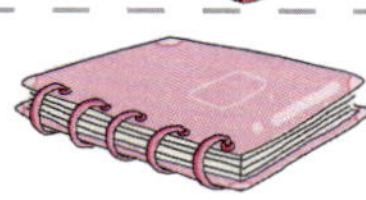	
	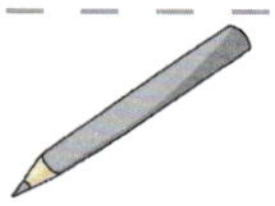	GOOD EVENING	GOODBYE
HELLO!	GOOD MORNING	GOOD AFTERNOON	GOOD NIGHT

Unit 3 • Lesson 12

1. LET'S PLAY *SIMON SAYS.*

LOOK!

2. COMPLETE

SIT ___ ___ ___ ___

STAND ___ ___

UP - DOWN

3. LET´S SING!

THE COLORS SONG

RED AND WHITE AND PINK AND GREEN

ORANGE AND BLACK AND BLUE

BROWN AND YELLOW,

BROWN AND YELLOW,

GRAY AND PURPLE TOO.

4. COLOR. USE THE COLORS FROM THE SONG.

VALUES
FOLLOW THE CLASSROOM RULES

Unit 3

1. COLOR THE PICTURE ACCORDING TO THE NUMBERS.

1	YELLOW
2	RED
3	BLUE
4	WHITE
5	GREEN

2. UNSCRAMBLE THE WORDS AND MATCH.

KINP ____________________

BCLKA ____________________

ORWBN ____________________

UPPRLE ____________________

RAGY ____________________

3. FIND 5 COLORS.

G	S	N	P	I	N	K	C
R	L	P	U	R	P	L	E
E	O	Y	E	L	L	O	W
E	K	L	H	L	O	P	Y
N	I	S	G	R	E	D	E

Unit 4 • Lesson 13

IT'S A TRIANGLE

1. LOOK, LISTEN AND SAY. 

IT'S A RECTANGLE.

IT'S A SQUARE.

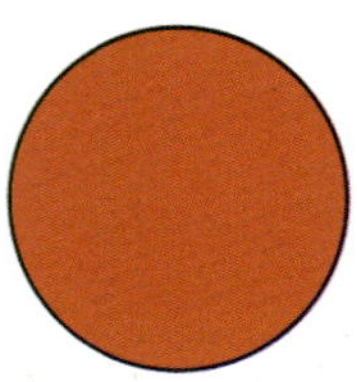

IT'S A CIRCLE.

IT'S A STAR.

2. STICK

IT'S A RED SQUARE.

IT'S A BLUE CIRCLE.

IT'S A YELLOW RECTANGLE.

IT'S A GREEN TRIANGLE.

IT'S A WHITE STAR.

LOOK!

3. MATCH AND WRITE.

__ __ __ __ __ __ __ __ __ __ __

COLOR - DRAW

Unit 4 • Lesson 14

1. LISTEN AND SAY. 

1 – ONE

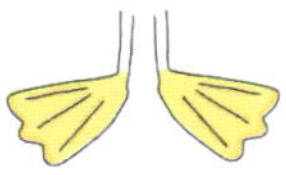

2 – TWO

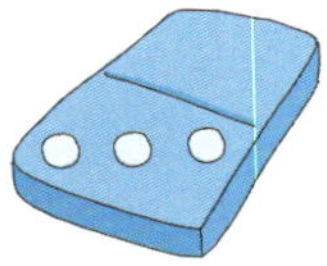

3 – THREE

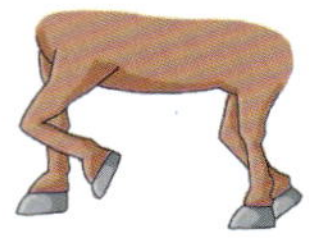

4 – FOUR

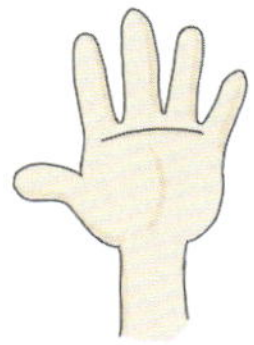

5 – FIVE

2. MATCH 

ONE RECTANGLE

TWO CIRCLES

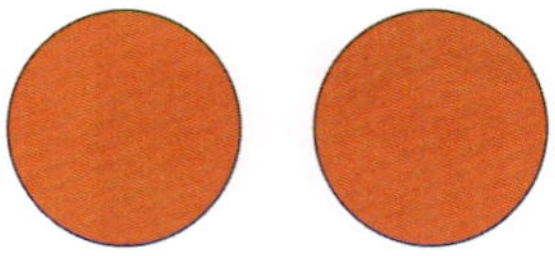

THREE TRIANGLES

FOUR SQUARES

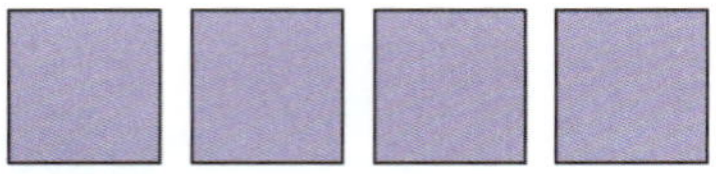

FIVE STARS

3. LISTEN AND COMPLETE.

4. LISTEN AND SAY.

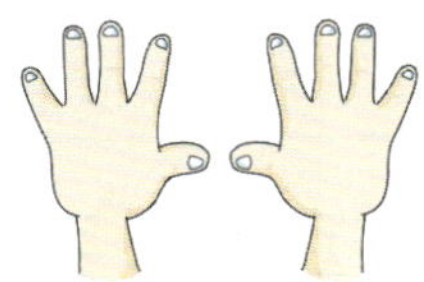

6 – SIX | 7 – SEVEN | 8 – EIGHT | 9 – NINE | 10 – TEN

Unit 4 • Lesson 15

1. LET´S SING!

SHOW ME!

SHOW ME ONE.
SHOW ME ONE.
ONE CIRCLE, ONE CIRCLE.
I SEE ONE, I SEE ONE.
ONE CIRCLE, ONE CIRCLE.

SHOW ME TWO.
SHOW ME TWO.
TWO SQUARES, TWO SQUARES.
I SEE TWO, I SEE TWO.
TWO SQUARES, TWO SQUARES.

SHOW ME THREE.
SHOW ME THREE.
THREE TRIANGLES, THREE TRIANGLES.
I SEE THREE, I SEE THREE.
THREE TRIANGLES, THREE TRIANGLES.

SHOW ME FOUR.
SHOW ME FOUR.
FOUR RECTANGLES, FOUR RECTANGLES.
I SEE FOUR, I SEE FOUR.
FOUR RECTANGLES, FOUR RECTANGLES.

2. COUNT AND CIRCLE.

ONE FOUR

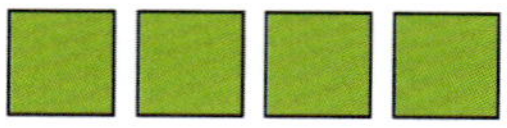

FOUR NINE

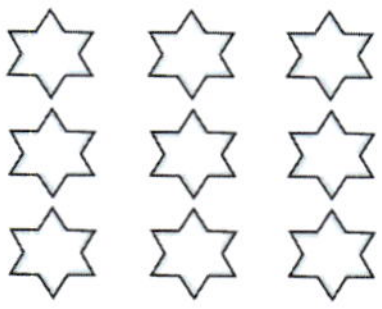

TWO NINE

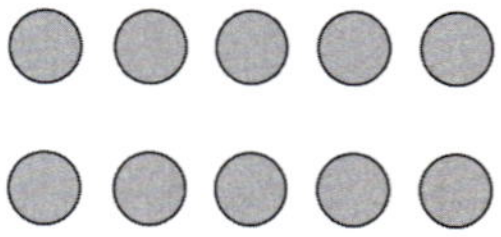

TEN THREE

EIGHT SIX

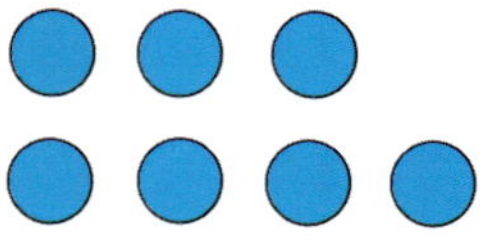

SEVEN TWO

FIVE THREE

TEN EIGHT

3. FIND AND COLOR.

- TWO CIRCLES
- THREE TRIANGLES
- FIVE SQUARES
- FOUR RECTANGLES
- SEVEN STARS
- NINE CIRCLES

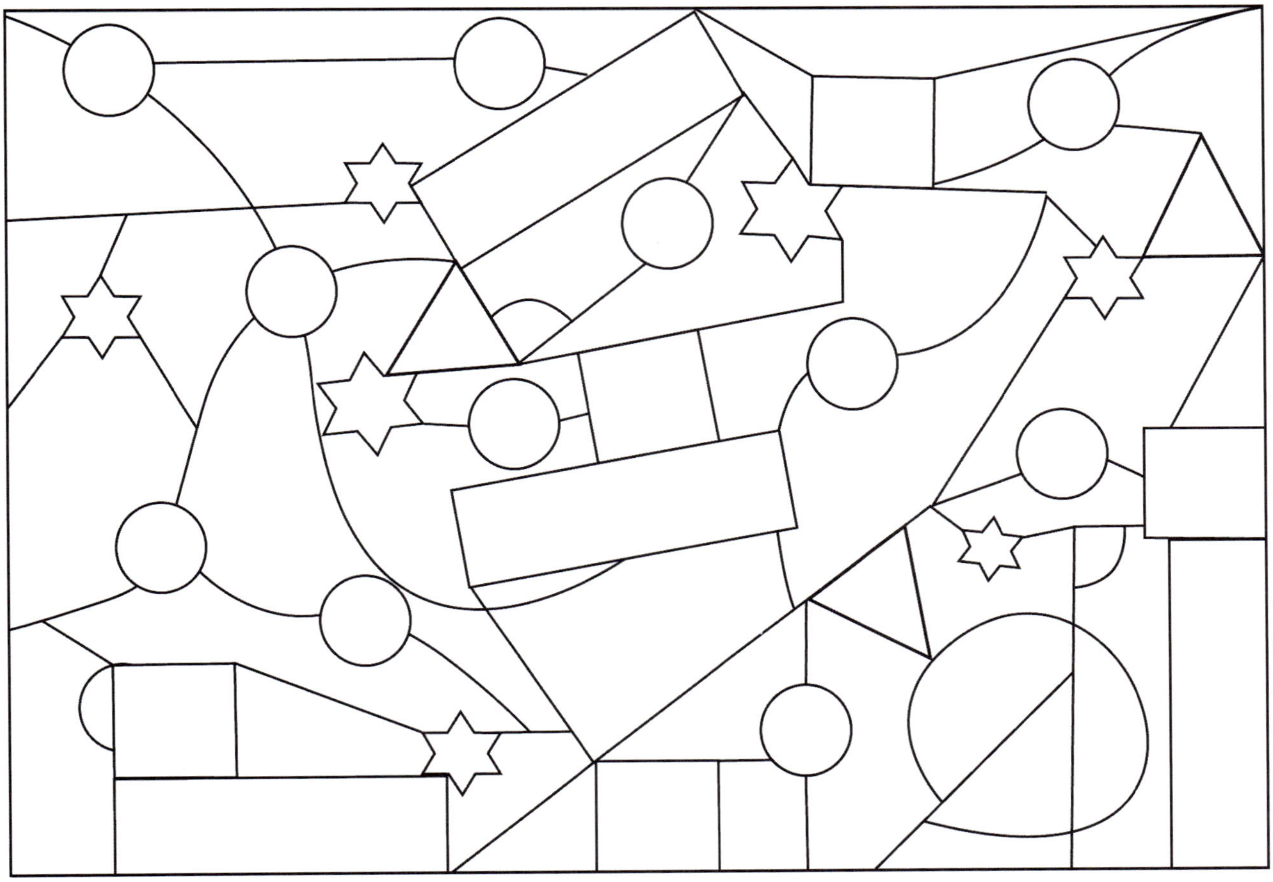

4. COUNT AND WRITE.

1.  O N E
2.  ___ ___ ___
3. 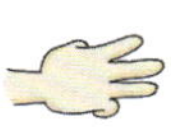 ___ ___ ___ ___ ___
4. 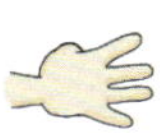 ___ ___ ___ ___
5. 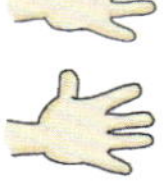 ___ ___ ___ ___

Unit 4 • Lesson 16

1. LISTEN, DRAW AND COLOR.

1

2

3

4

2. SOLVE AND WRITE.

a) 7 + 2 = ___ ___ ___ ___ ___

b) 4 + 3 = ___ ___ ___ ___ ___ ___

c) 5 + 1 = ___ ___ ___ ___

d) 9 + 1 = ___ ___ ___ ___

e) 4 + 4 = ___ ___ ___ ___ ___ ___

3. CROSSWORD

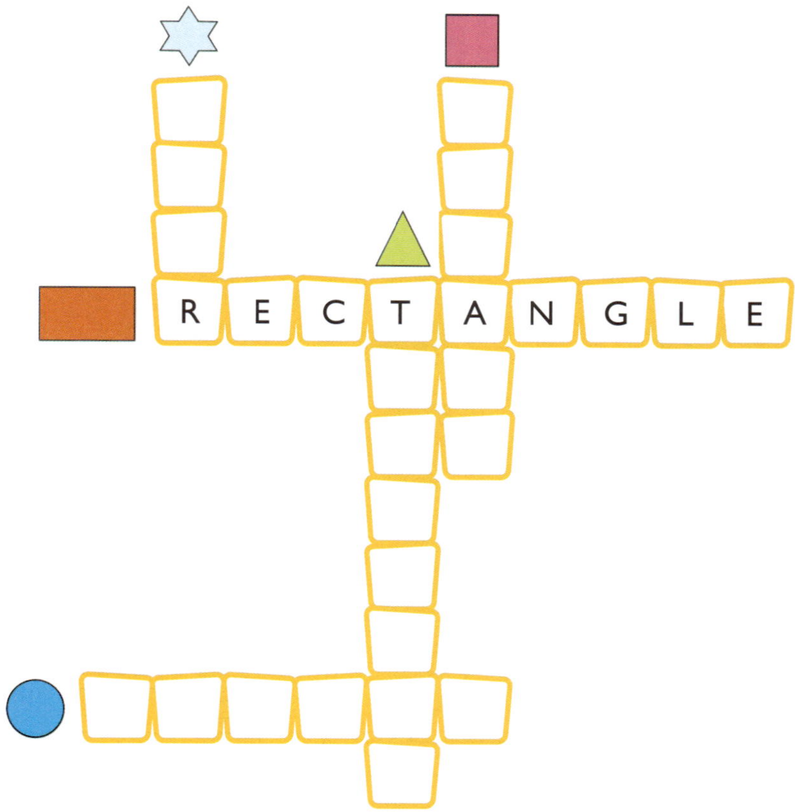

PROJECT

CREATE YOUR OWN PAPER ROBOT.

EXTRA WORK

Unit 4

1. DECORATE YOUR PICTURE.

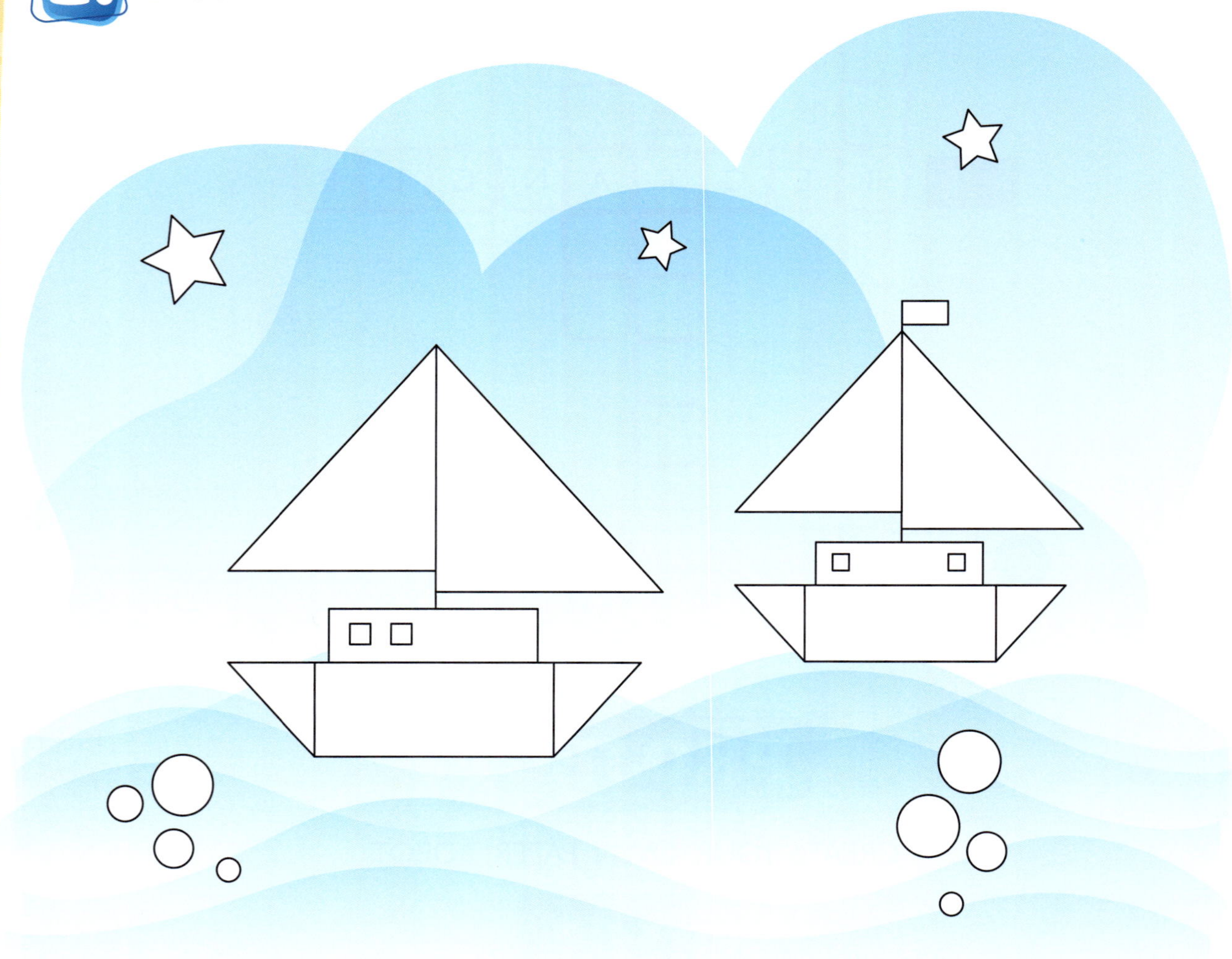

2. NOW, COUNT AND COMPLETE.

3	STARS
___	SQUARES
___	CIRCLES
___	RECTANGLES
___	TRIANGLES

3. MATCH

ONE

TWO

THREE

FOUR

FIVE

SIX

SEVEN

EIGHT

NINE

TEN

Units 1-4 • Review

GAME:

SNAKES AND LADDERS

35
YOUR BOOK
34 WHAT IS IT?
33 WHAT COLOR IS IT?
32 WHAT'S MY NAME?
31
G
N
27
GOOD
28
29 WHAT'S THE NUMBER?
7
30 GOOD
15 WHAT COLOR IS IT?
14 WHAT COLOR IS IT?
13 WHAT SHAPE IS IT?
12
L
11
WHAT'S MY NAME?
6 WHAT'S THE NUMBER?
10
7 WHAT SHAPE IS IT?
8 WHAT COLOR IS IT?
9 WHAT IS IT?
10 WHAT'S THE NUMBER?
3

Unit 5 • Lesson 17

PARTS OF THE BODY

1. LOOK, LISTEN AND SAY.

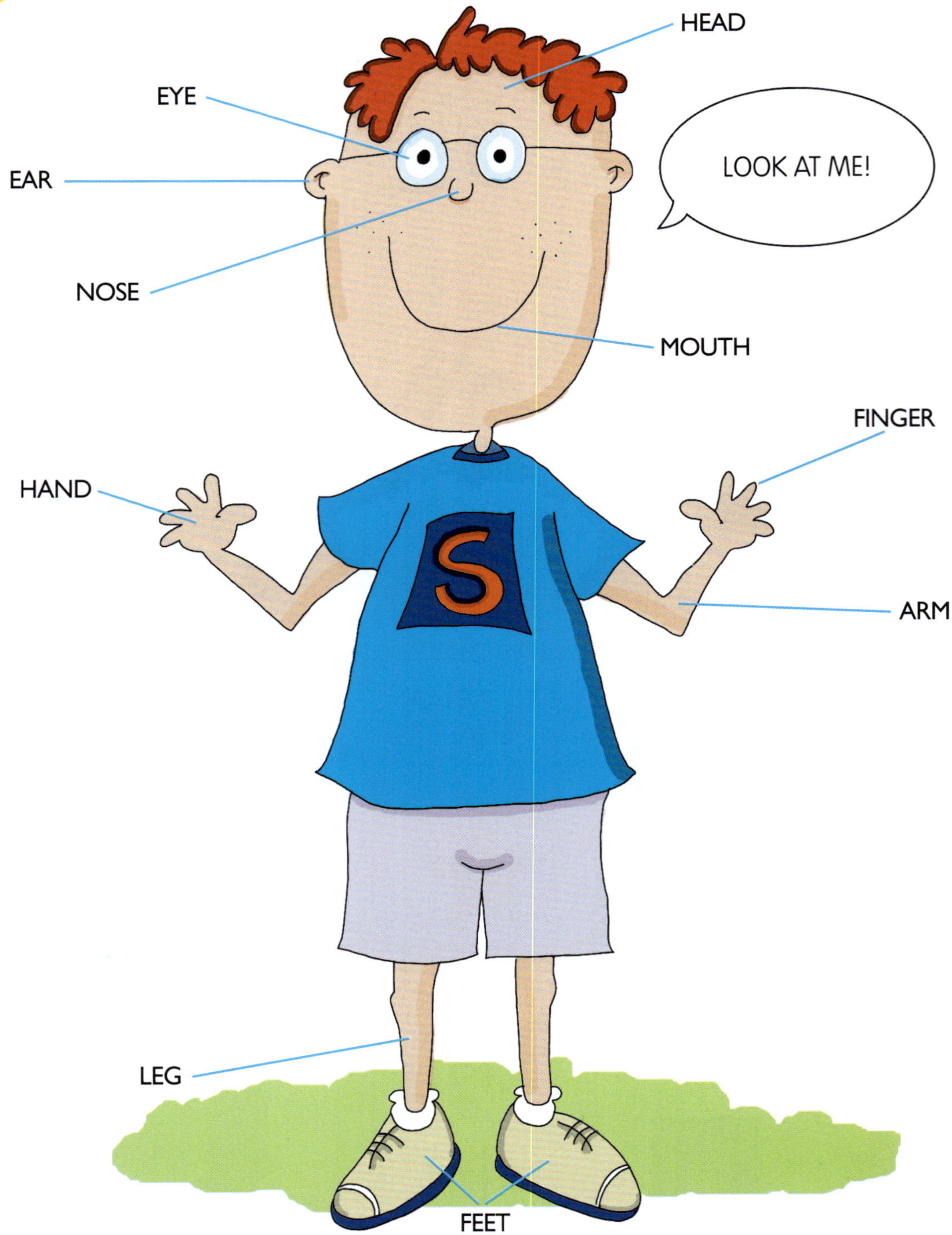

2. MAKE AN X.

1	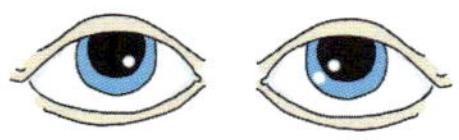	NOSE	☐	EYES	X
2	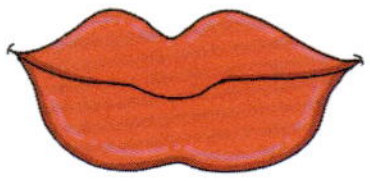	MOUTH	☐	HEAD	☐
3	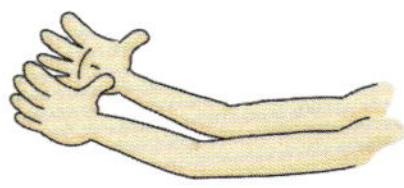	FEET	☐	ARMS	☐
4	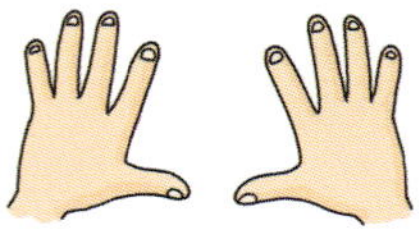	EARS	☐	HANDS	☐
5		HEAD	☐	NOSE	☐
6	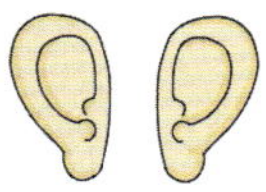	HANDS	☐	EARS	☐

3. LET´S SING!

HEAD AND SHOULDERS, KNEES AND TOES

HEAD AND SHOULDERS,
HEAD AND SHOULDERS,
KNEES AND TOES, KNEES AND TOES.

HEAD AND SHOULDERS,
HEAD AND SHOULDERS,
KNEES AND TOES, KNEES AND TOES.

EYES AND EARS, EYES AND EARS,
MOUTH AND NOSE, MOUTH AND NOSE. } X 2

Unit 5 • Lesson 18

1. LOOK AT THE ANIMALS. PUT YES (Y) OR NO (N).

FISH

N LEGS
___ EYES
___ MOUTH
___ FEET
___ ARMS
___ HANDS

SNAKE

___ ARMS
___ HEAD
___ EYES
___ FEET
___ LEGS
___ HANDS

MONKEY

___ ARMS
___ HANDS
___ HEAD
___ EARS
___ FINGERS
___ FEET

HORSE

___ LEGS
___ HEAD
___ EARS
___ FINGERS
___ EYES
___ HANDS

2. READ AND CIRCLE.

THE HEAD IS	GRAY /	BLACK /	PINK.
THE EYES ARE	GREEN /	BLUE /	BROWN.
THE BODY IS	WHITE /	BLUE /	BLACK.
THE LEGS ARE	RED /	BLACK /	GRAY.

3. FIND NINE PARTS OF THE BODY.

Unit 5 • Lesson 19

1. FIND AND WRITE THE WORDS.

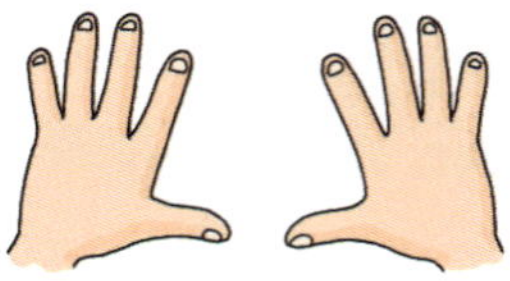

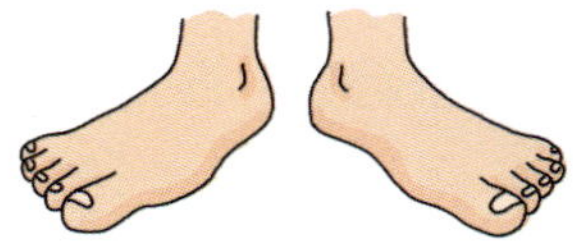

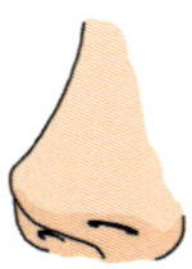

P	F	Y	A	E	W	E	W
E	E	E	R	A	P	Y	D
R	E	H	H	R	I	E	F
M	T	A	D	S	L	S	S
O	P	N	X	C	K	K	G
U	K	D	A	R	M	S	C
T	L	S	S	V	M	U	N
H	M	U	Z	B	A	I	O
F	A	N	I	E	R	O	S
I	H	E	A	D	N	N	E
P	H	B	C	D	W	O	A
U	Y	T	E	Q	S	X	W
L	E	G	S	Y	W	T	E

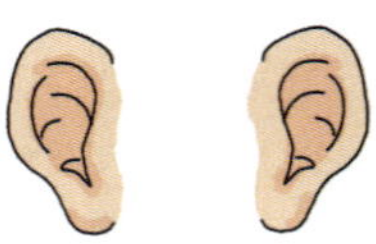

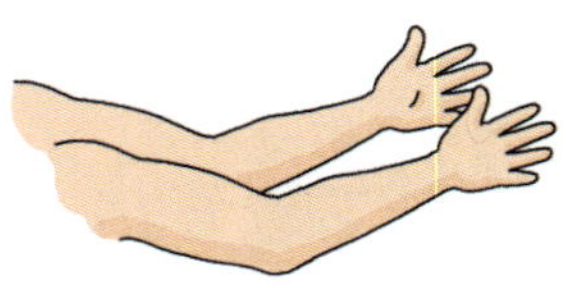

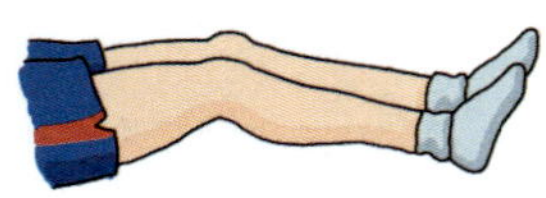

2. COMPLETE THE ROBOT, COLOR AND WRITE ABOUT IT.

THE ROBOT:

___1___ MOUTH

______ EYES

______ NOSE

______ LEGS

______ HANDS

______ FINGERS

______ FEET

3. PLAY A MEMORY GAME!

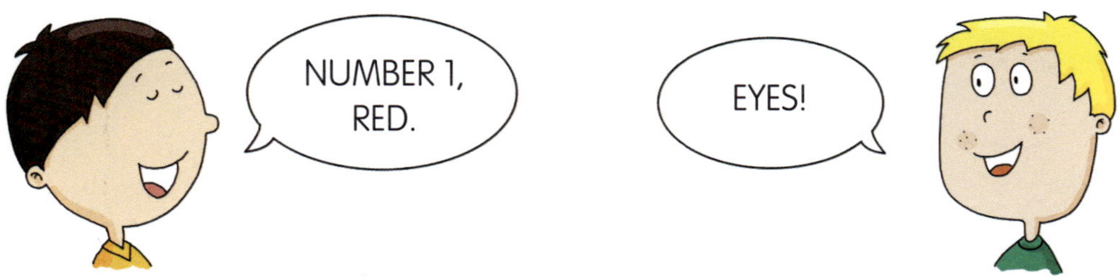

1.		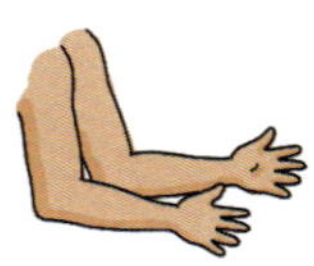	
2	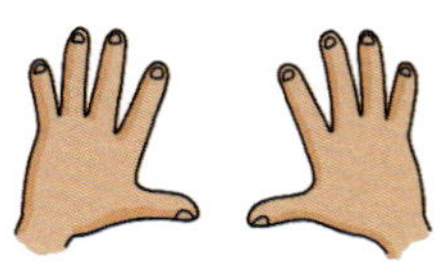	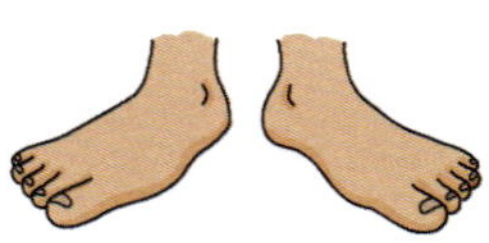	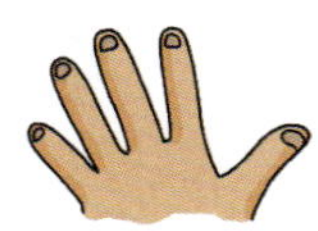
3.	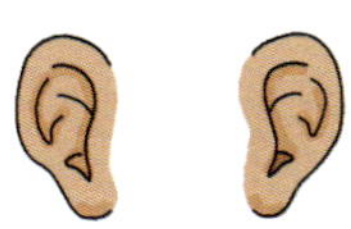		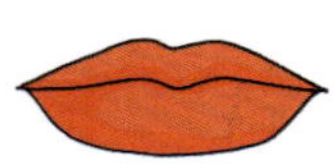

Unit 5 • Lesson 20

1. LISTEN AND CIRCLE.

1. 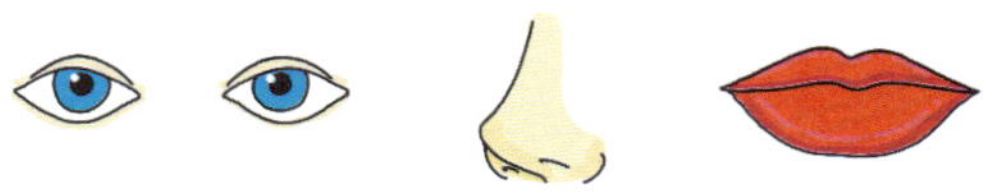

2. 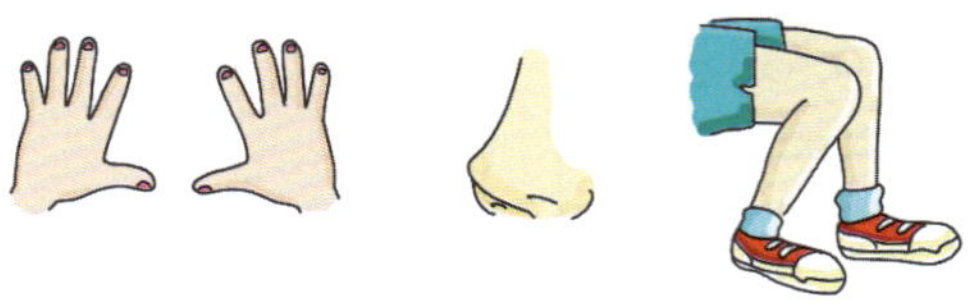

3. 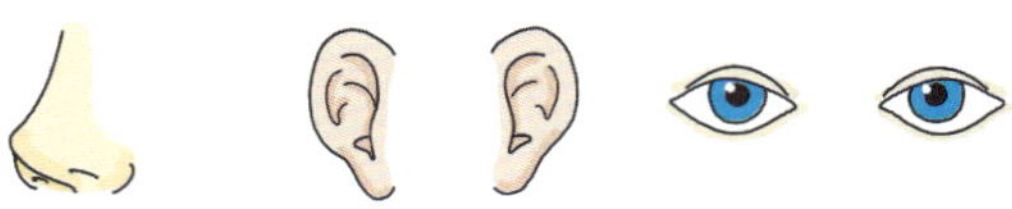

4. 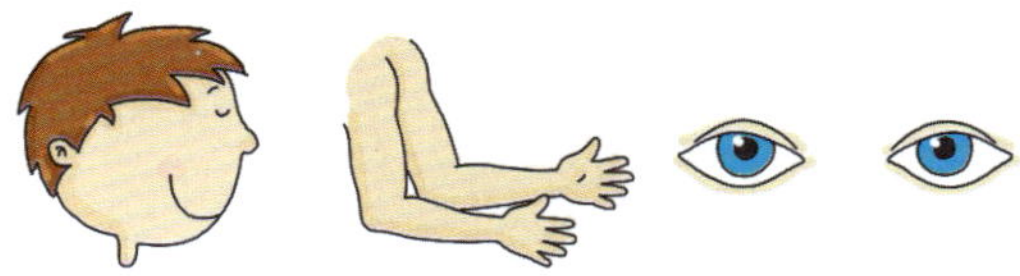

5. 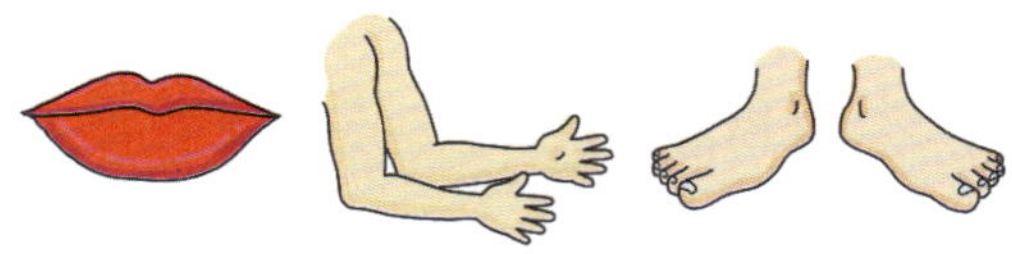

6. 

LOOK!

2. COLOR AND WRITE.

T___ ___ ___ ___

P ___ ___ ___ ___

TOUCH - POINT

3. UNSCRAMBLE THE WORDS AND MATCH.

1. E E Y S ______________________

2. E A H D ______________________

3. O S N E ______________________

4. S A R E ______________________

5. E S G L ______________________

6. M U T O H ______________________

7. N H D A S ______________________

8. F T E E ______________________

EXTRA WORK

1. LABEL THE PARTS OF THE BODY.

HEAD EYES LEG NOSE MOUTH ARM EAR

2. NOW, COLOR THE PICTURE.

3. READ AND CUT PICTURES FROM MAGAZINES.

TWO ARMS

ONE LEG

BLUE EYES

ONE HEAD

A RED MOUTH

FOUR EARS

Unit 6 • Lesson 21

THIS IS MY PET!

1. LISTEN, POINT AND SAY.

2. LISTEN AND STICK

1.
2.
3.
4.
5.
6.

WHAT IS YOUR FAVORITE PET? ______________________

3. FIND OUT AND CIRCLE.

A	B	C	D	E	F	G	H	I	J	K	L	M
👁	👍	👂	♥	❑	❄	◆	☺	☽	✋	✿	☹	★
N	**O**	**P**	**Q**	**R**	**S**	**T**	**U**	**V**	**W**	**X**	**Y**	**Z**
✪	✲	✌	✻	●	✤	⌘	✱	✺	▲	☐	❖	💣

1. 👂 👁 ⌘ ______________

2. ♥ ✲ ◆ ______________

3. ◆ ✲ ☹ ♥ ❄ ☽ ✤ ☺ ______________

4. ☺ 👁 ★ ✤ ⌘ ❑ ● ______________

5. ⌘ ✱ ● ⌘ ☹ ❑ ______________

6. ● 👁 👍 👍 ☽ ⌘ ______________

Unit 6 • Lesson 22

1. LISTEN AND READ.

VALUES
BE KIND TO PETS

2. ANSWER "YES, IT IS" OR "NO, IT ISN'T".

IS IT A CAT?

____

IS IT A TURTLE?

____

IS IT A HAMSTER?

____

IS IT A FISH?

____

IS IT A DOG?

____

IS IT A RABBIT?

____

3. LET´S SING!

MY NAME IS LITTLE YELLOW BIRD

MY NAME IS LITTLE YELLOW BIRD,

YELLOW BIRD, YELLOW BIRD,

MY NAME IS LITTLE YELLOW BIRD,

AND WHO ARE YOU?

4. COUNT THE SHAPES.

1.

CIRCLES	1
TRIANGLES	
STARS	
RECTANGLES	
SQUARES	

2.

SQUARES	
CIRCLES	
RECTANGLES	
TRIANGLES	
STARS	

3.

TRIANGLES	
RECTANGLES	
CIRCLES	
SQUARES	
STARS	

1. JOIN THE DOTS AND WRITE.

1

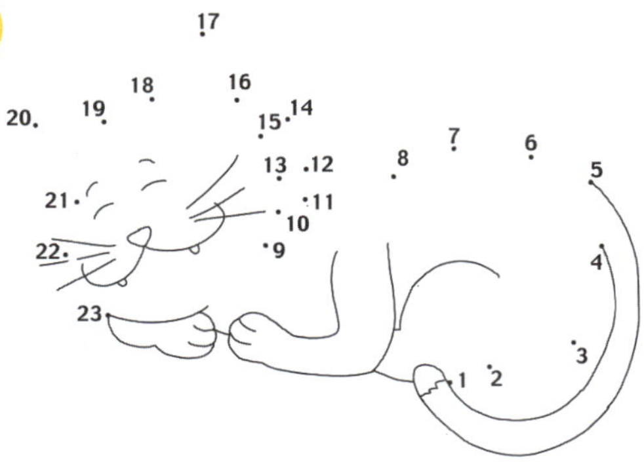

IT'S A ______________________

2

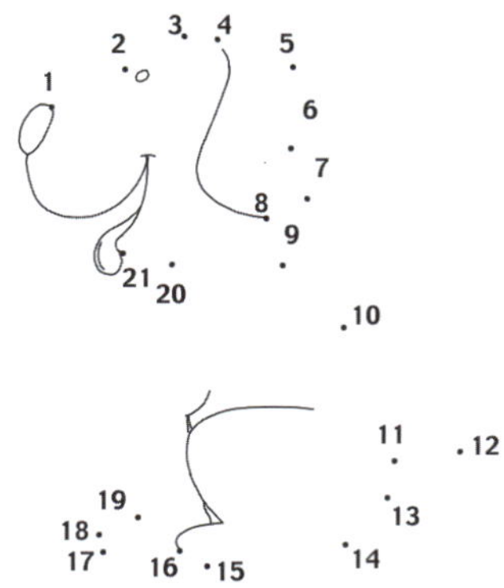

IT'S A ______________________

3

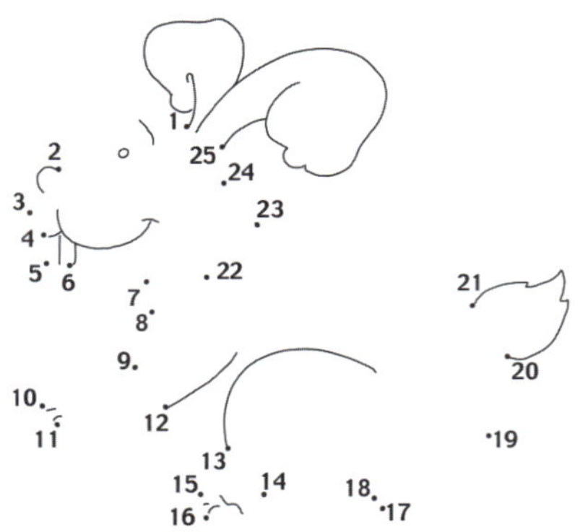

IT'S A ______________________

4

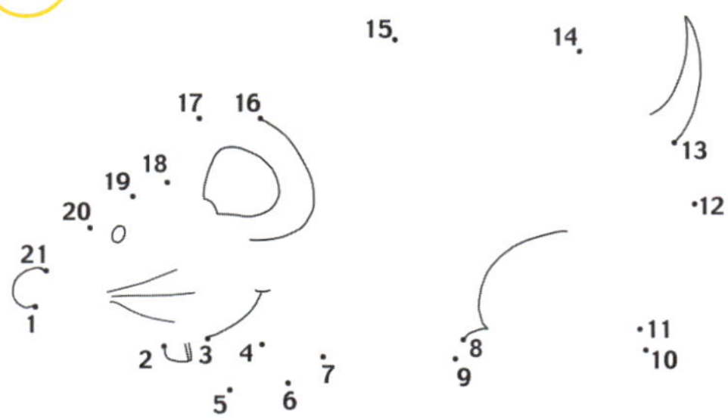

IT'S A ______________________

5

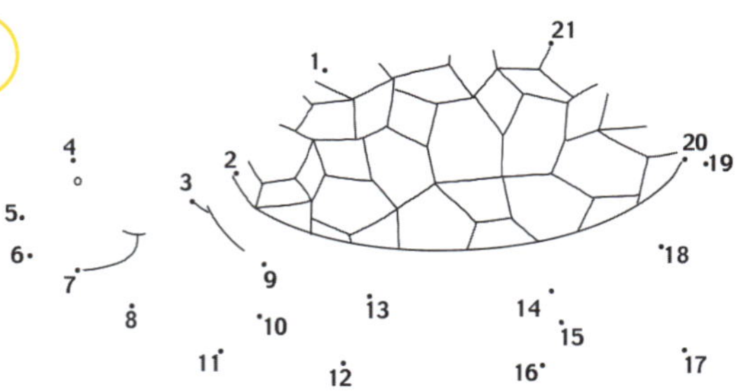

IT'S A ______________________

6

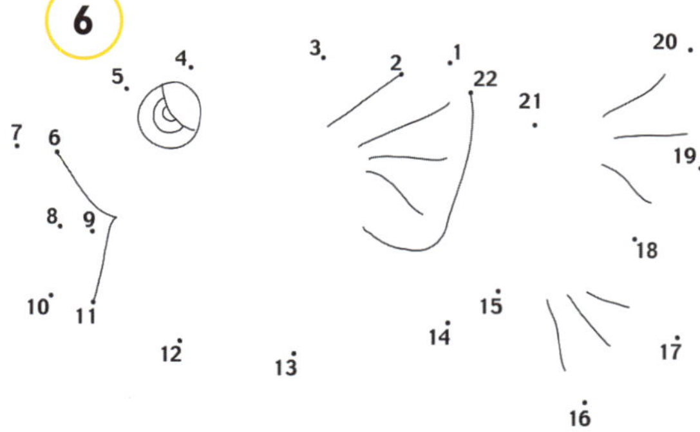

IT'S A ______________________

2. COLOR

1. 1 ORANGE FISH

2. 3 BLUE BIRDS

3. 6 YELLOW CATS

4. 7 GREEN TURTLES

3. LISTEN AND CHECK.

		YES	NO
1.			
2.			
3.			

		YES	NO
4.			
5.			
6.			

Unit 6 • Lesson 24

1. COLOR THE PETS.

POINT TO THE ANIMALS AND ASK YOUR FRIEND:

WHAT COLOR IS IT?

LOOK!

2. LOOK AND WRITE.

______________________ ______________________

BE QUIET - PAY ATTENTION

3. CROSSWORD

PROJECT

CREATE A POSTER.

EXTRA WORK

Unit 6

1. COMPLETE THE DRAWINGS AND MATCH.

CAT

TURTLE

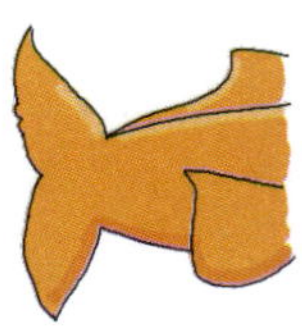

GOLDFISH

BIRD

RABBIT

2. JOIN THE DOTS AND COLOR.

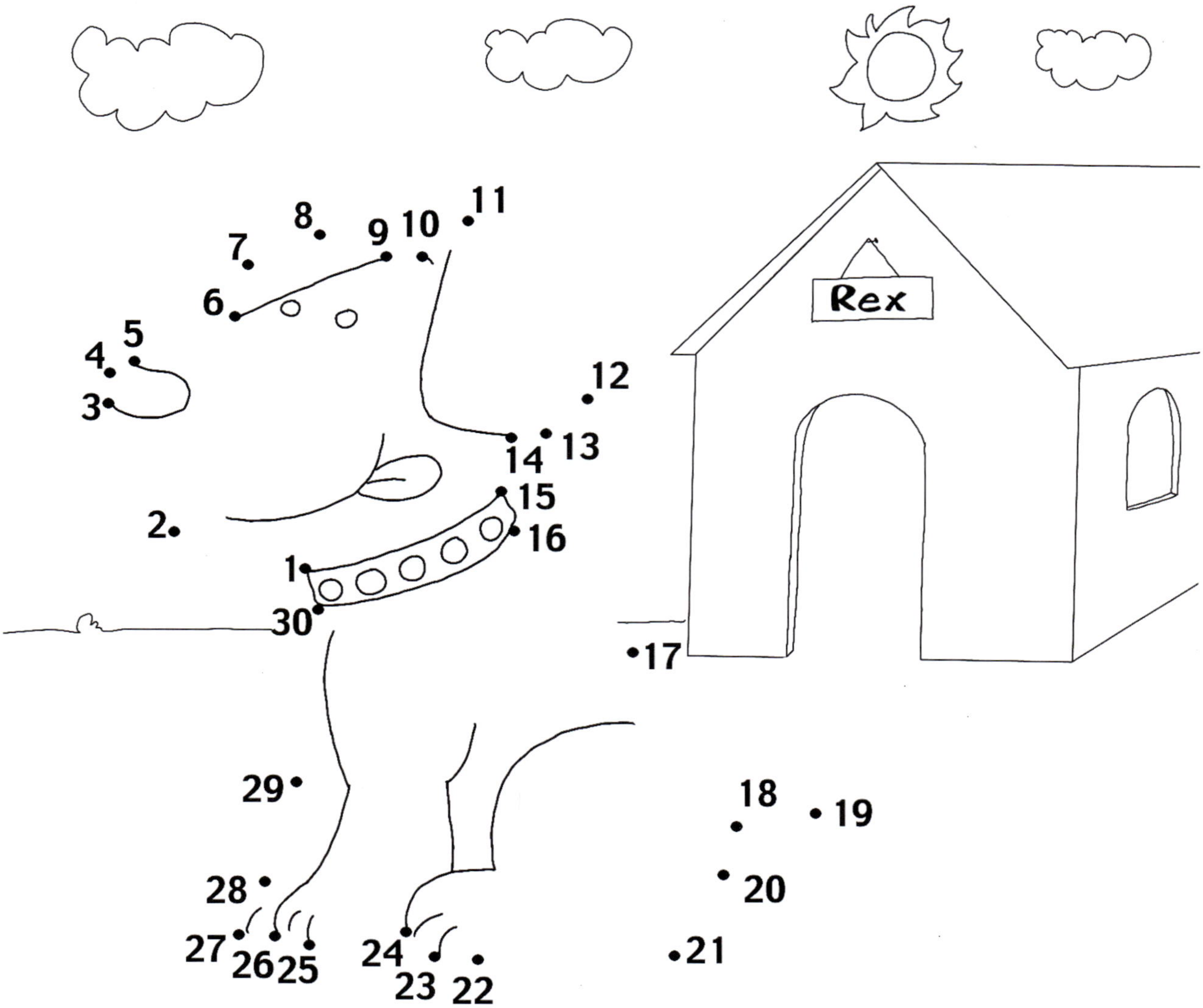

WHAT IS IT? IT'S A ______________________________

Unit 7 • Lesson 25

MY NEW TOYS

1. LISTEN, POINT AND SAY.

2. CIRCLE THE CORRECT PICTURE

1. IT'S A PINK DOLLHOUSE.  

2. IT'S A BLUE BIKE.  

3. IT'S A RED BALL.  

4. IT'S A GREEN SKATEBOARD.  

5. IT'S A WHITE TEDDY BEAR.  

6. IT'S A BLACK ROBOT.  

3. STICK AND WRITE.

1 IT'S A ______________________

2 ______________________

3 ______________________

4 ______________________

Unit 7 • Lesson 26

1. LOOK AND CIRCLE. 

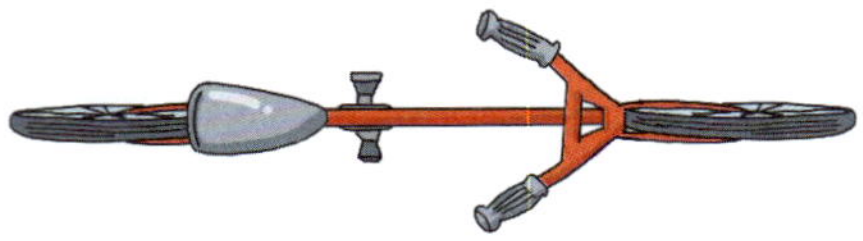

1. IS IT A BIKE?

YES, IT IS.
NO, IT ISN'T.

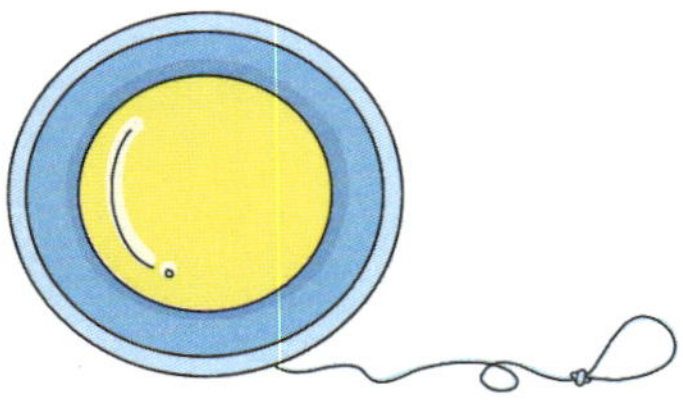

2. IS IT A YO-YO?

YES, IT IS.
NO, IT ISN'T.

3. IS IT A DOLL?

YES, IT IS.
NO, IT ISN'T.

4. IS IT A SKATEBOARD?

YES, IT IS.
NO, IT ISN'T.

5. IS IT A VIDEO GAME?

YES, IT IS.
NO, IT ISN'T.

2. COUNT AND WRITE.

2 BIKES

3. LOOK AND COMPLETE.

RED TOYS	5
ORANGE TOYS	
BLUE TOYS	

PINK TOYS	
YELLOW TOYS	
GREEN TOYS	

Unit 7 • Lesson 27

1. LET´S SING!

TEDDY BEAR, TEDDY BEAR

I LOVE MY TEDDY BEAR.
I LOVE MY TEDDY BEAR.
I KISS TEDDY EVERY NIGHT.
TEDDY BEAR, TEDDY BEAR,
SLEEP TIGHT.
LOVE, LOVE, LOVE, LOVE
TEDDY, I LOVE YOU.
LOVE, LOVE, LOVE, LOVE
TEDDY LOVES ME, TOO.

2. LISTEN AND CIRCLE.

1. 

2. 

3. 

4. 

5. 

6. 

3. DRAW AND TALK. 

4. FIND AND CLASSIFY THE WORDS. 

P	S	P	D	P	E	N	O	T	W	B	R	Q	Q	M
R	A	A	O	R	R	R	E	J	A	H	T	A	D	P
G	Z	R	T	F	E	A	E	K	Z	O	E	H	S	E
B	X	D	O	G	C	P	C	L	D	O	D	U	A	N
V	D	O	U	G	V	I	P	M	F	L	D	I	Q	C
B	T	T	B	G	T	L	A	R	M	J	Y	L	Q	I
N	Q	P	I	I	U	U	F	O	Y	M	#	M	D	L
M	Y	O	K	I	R	T	V	L	U	T	B	N	F	J
O	U	I	E	O	T	G	R	I	I	G	E	N	G	K
C	I	L	L	L	L	B	E	O	L	F	A	O	U	L
W	L	B	Y	P	E	V	A	O	I	P	R	R	M	B
R	P	B	R	Y	E	C	X	P	L	E	L	S	J	E
U	O	I	I	T	D	O	L	L	P	D	W	E	J	P
L	O	P	U	Z	Z	L	E	Q	W	U	S	I	K	I
C	Q	N	O	T	E	B	O	O	K	Y	C	A	T	Q

PETS	SCHOOL OBJECTS	TOYS
	PEN	

Unit 7 • Lesson 28

1. TIC-TAC-TOE

LOOK!

2. MATCH

I WIN! - YOUR TURN

3. LET'S PLAY BINGO!

DRAW THE PICTURES AND LET'S PLAY.

BOOK	HEAD	BIRD	BALL	SCHOOLBAG
BIKE	PENCIL	YO-YO	TRIANGLE	TEDDY BEAR
CRAYON	DOLL	DOG	SKATEBOARD	HAMSTER
LEGS	NOSE	SQUARE	CIRCLE	ARMS
ROBOT	FISH	CAT	NOTEBOOK	DOLLHOUSE

1. WHERE ARE THEY?

A DOLL • A TEDDY BEAR • A BALL • A YO-YO • A VIDEO GAME

2. WRITE THE NUMBERS AND COMPLETE THE PICTURES.

1 ONE

_____ TWO

_____ THREE

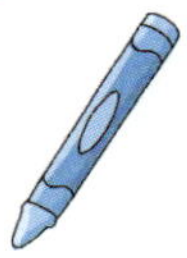

_____ FOUR

_____ FIVE

_____ SIX

_____ SEVEN

_____ EIGHT

_____ NINE

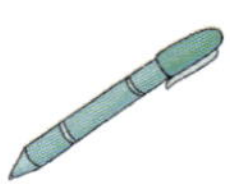

_____ TEN

Unit 8 • Lesson 29

THIS IS MY FAMILY

1. LISTEN AND REPEAT.

2. FIND THE STICKERS.

VALUES
LISTEN TO MOM AND DAD

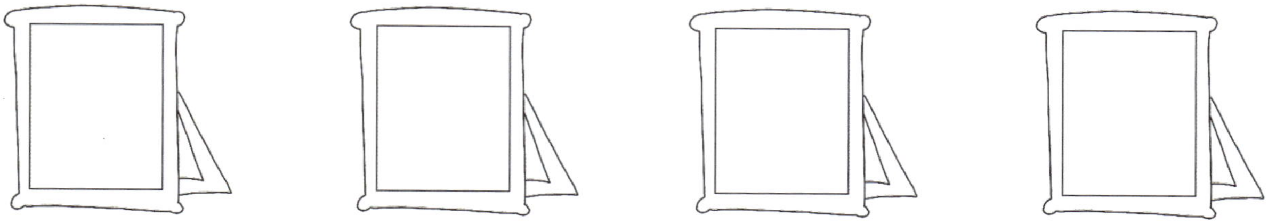

FATHER MOTHER BROTHER SISTER

GRANDMOTHER GRANDFATHER

3. LISTEN AND CHECK (✔).

1. FATHER ( ) BROTHER ( ) GRANDFATHER ( )
2. MOTHER ( ) BROTHER ( ) SISTER ( )
3. GRANDFATHER ( ) FATHER ( ) BROTHER ( )
4. MOTHER ( ) GRANDMOTHER ( ) SISTER ( )
5. MOTHER ( ) GRANDMOTHER ( ) GRANDFATHER ( )
6. SISTER ( ) GRANDMOTHER ( ) FATHER ( )

1. COMPLETE THE SENTENCES.

1. HE IS ______________________________

2. SHE IS ______________________________

3. HE IS ______________________________

4. SHE IS ______________________________

5. SHE IS ______________________________

6. HE IS ______________________________

1

2

3

4

5

6

2. CIRCLE THE CORRECT WORD.

1.  HE / SHE

4.  HE / SHE

2.  HE / SHE

5.  HE / SHE

3.  HE / SHE

6.  HE / SHE

3. GLUE A PICTURE OF YOUR FAMILY OR DRAW IT.

4. TALK TO YOUR FRIEND.

Unit 8 • Lesson 31

1. THIS IS FRANCISCO'S FAMILY. CIRCLE THE CORRECT WORD.

JOANA

MOTHER / GRANDMOTHER

CARLOS

FATHER / GRANDFATHER

LUÍSA

BROTHER / SISTER

JOAQUIM

FATHER / BROTHER

TEREZA

GRANDMOTHER / MOTHER

JOSÉ

GRANDFATHER / FATHER

2. COMPLETE THE SENTENCES.

1. CARLOS IS MY ____________________
2. JOANA IS MY ____________________
3. JOAQUIM IS MY ____________________
4. LUÍSA IS MY ____________________
5. JOSÉ IS MY ____________________
6. TEREZA IS MY ____________________

3. LET'S SING!

I LOVE MY FAMILY

I LOVE MY MOTHER,
AND MY MOTHER LOVES ME!
I LOVE MY FATHER,
AND MY FATHER LOVES ME!
LOVE, LOVE, LOVE, LOVE, } X 2
I LOVE MY FAMILY! }
I LOVE MY SISTER,
AND MY SISTER LOVES ME!
I LOVE MY BROTHER,
AND MY BROTHER LOVES ME!
LOVE, LOVE, LOVE, LOVE, } X 2
I LOVE MY FAMILY. }

4. LOOK AT LUCIANA'S FAMILY. COLOR AND WRITE:

FATHER / MOTHER / GRANDMOTHER / BROTHER

1. COMPLETE THE SENTENCES.

WHO IS JORGE?

HE IS MY GRANDFATHER.

WHO IS ELISA?

_____ IS MY GRANDMOTHER.

WHO IS ANITA?

_____ IS MY MOTHER.

WHO IS RICARDO?

HE IS ____________________

WHO IS ROBERTO?

_____ IS MY BROTHER.

WHO IS CLÁUDIA?

____

2. READING TIME

LOOK!

3. COMPLETE

_ _ _ _ _ YOUR HAND

_ _ _ _ YOUR HANDS

RAISE - CLAP

EXTRA WORK

Unit 8

1. LOOK FOR PICTURES IN A MAGAZINE AND COMPLETE THE CHART.

HE
SHE

2. LOOK IN A MAGAZINE AND CUT OUT A PICTURE OF A FAMILY. THEN WRITE.

MOTHER FATHER SISTER
BROTHER GRANDMOTHER GRANDFATHER

Units 5-8 • Review

1. RACE GAME

STUDENT A	STUDENT B
START	**START**
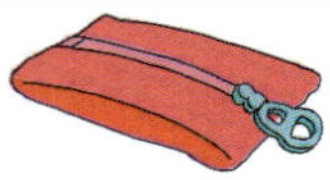	

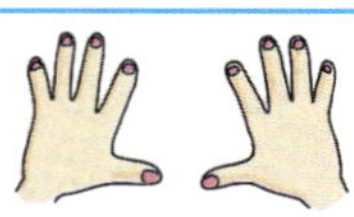	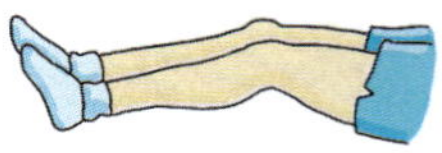

	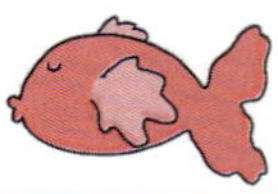

FINISH	**FINISH**

STUDENT C
START
FINISH

STUDENT D
START
FINISH

Word List

A

animal – animal
another – outro(a)
answer – responder
arms – braços
ask – perguntar

B

ball – bola
be quiet – fique quieto(a)
beautiful – bonito(a)
bike – bicicleta
bird – passarinho
black – preto(a)
blue – azul
body – corpo
book – livro
both – ambos(as)
brother – irmão
brown – marrom
bye-bye – tchau

C

cat – gato
circle – círculo; circular
clap your hands – bater palmas
classify – classificar
close – fechar
code – código
color – cor; colorir
complete – completar
count – contar
crayon – lápis de cera
create – criar
crossword – palavras cruzadas
cut – cortar
check – verificar

D

dog – cachorro(a)
doll – boneca
dollhouse – casa de boneca
dots – pontos
down – para baixo
draw – desenhar

E

ears – orelhas
eight – oito
everybody – todos
eyes – olhos

F

family – família
family tree – árvore genealógica
father – pai
favorite – favorito(a)
feet – pés
find – achar
find out – descobrir
fingers – dedos
finish – terminar
fish – peixe
five – cinco
four – quarto
friend – amigo(a)

G

game – jogo
glue – colar

go – ir
goldfish – peixinho dourado
good afternoon – boa tarde
good evening – boa noite
good morning – bom dia
good night – boa noite
goodbye – tchau, até logo
grandfather – avô
grandmother – avó
gray – cinza
green – verde

H

hands – mãos
head – cabeça
help – ajuda; ajudar
hello – olá, alô, oi
hi – olá, alô, oi
horse – cavalo
How are you? – Como vai você?

I

I'm fine – Estou bem.

J

join – ligar, juntar

K

kiss – beijar

L

legs – pernas
Let's sing! – Vamos cantar!
listen – ouvir
little – pequeno(a)
look – olhar
love – amar

M

match – combinar
memory – memória
miss a turn – perder a vez (de jogar)
monkey – macaco
mother – mãe
mouth – boca
my – meu, minha

N

name – nome
new – novo(a)
nine – nove
no – não
nose – nariz
notebook – caderno

O

objects – objetos
one – um(a)
open – abrir
own – próprio(a)

P

paper – papel
parts – partes
pay attention – preste(m) atenção
pen – caneta
pencil – lápis
pencil case – estojo de lápis
pencil sharpener – apontador de lápis
pet – animal doméstico
pink – rosa
play – brincar; jogar
please – por favor
point – apontar

poster – cartaz
project – projeto
purple – roxo(a)
put – pôr; colocar

R

rabbit – coelho
rainbow – arco-íris
raise – erguer; levantar
read – ler
rectangle – retângulo
red – vermelho(a)
robot – robô
ruler – régua

S

say – dizer
school – escola
schoolbag – mochila escolar
see – ver
seven – sete
shake – sacudir, agitar
shapes – formas, figuras
show – mostrar
sing – cantar
sister – irmã
sit down – sentar-se
six – seis
sleep – dormir
snake – cobra
solve – resolver
square – quadrado
stand up – levantar-se
star – estrela

T

take – tomar, pegar
talk – conversar
teacher – professor(a)
teddy bear – ursinho de pelúcia
ten – dez
this – este; esta
three – três
too – também
touch – tocar
toy – brinquedo
triangle – triângulo
turn – virar
turtle – tartaruga
two – dois; duas

U

up – para cima

W

what – qual; o que
what is it? – O que é isto?
white – branco(a)
who – quem
whole – inteiro(a); todo(a)
win – vencer
word – palavra
write – escrever
wrong – errado(a)

Y

yellow – amarelo(a)
yes – sim
your – seu; sua
your turn – sua vez

Spaghetti Kids

EDIÇÃO ATUALIZADA

Special Projects

A Card

YOU NEED:

STEPS:

2

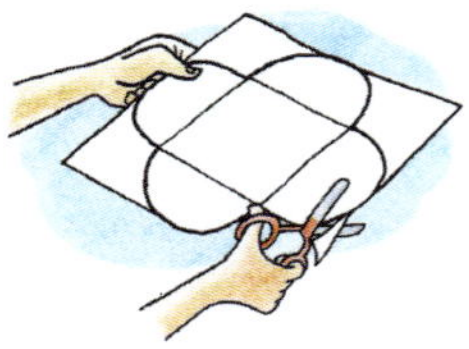

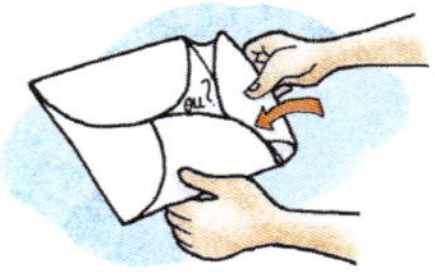

3

1

4

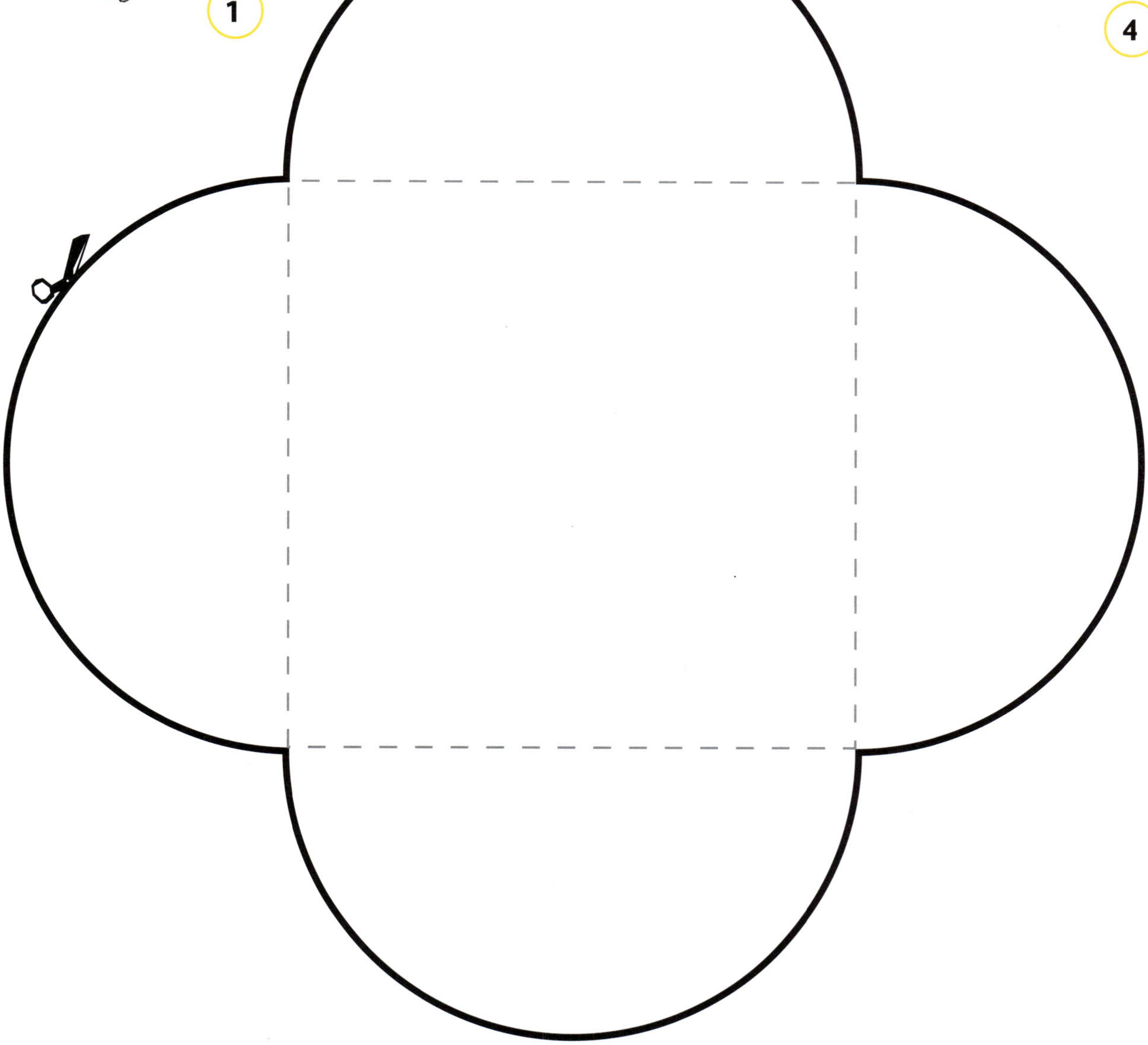

A Puppy

YOU NEED:

STEPS:

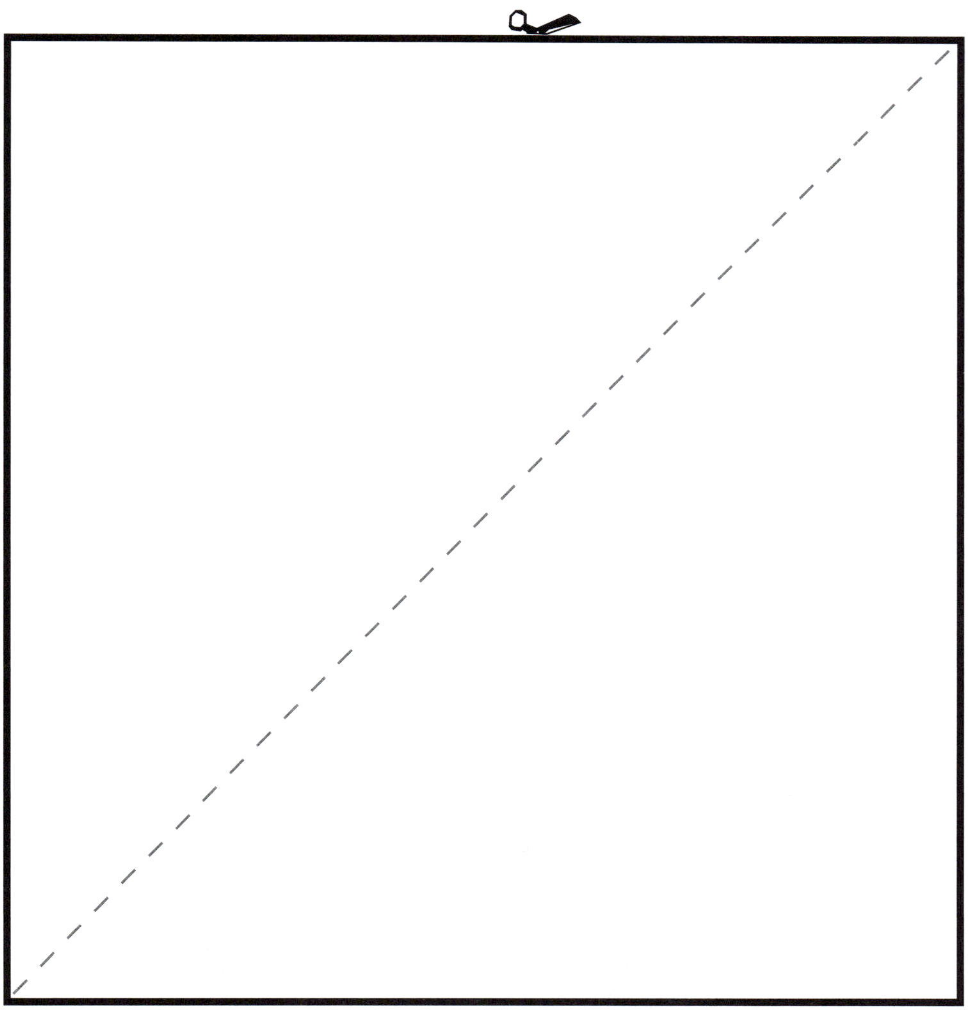

A Star

YOU NEED:

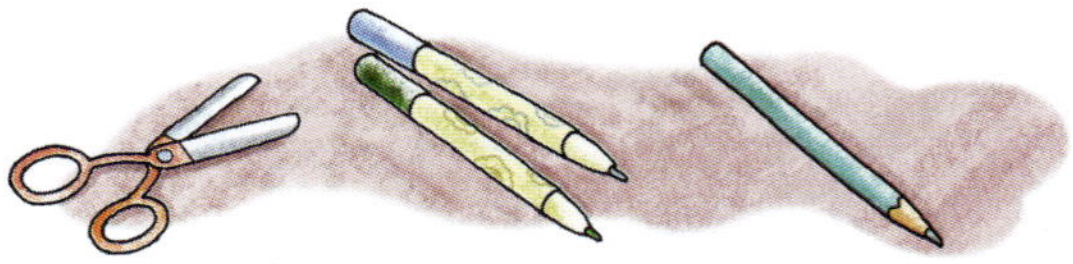

STEPS:

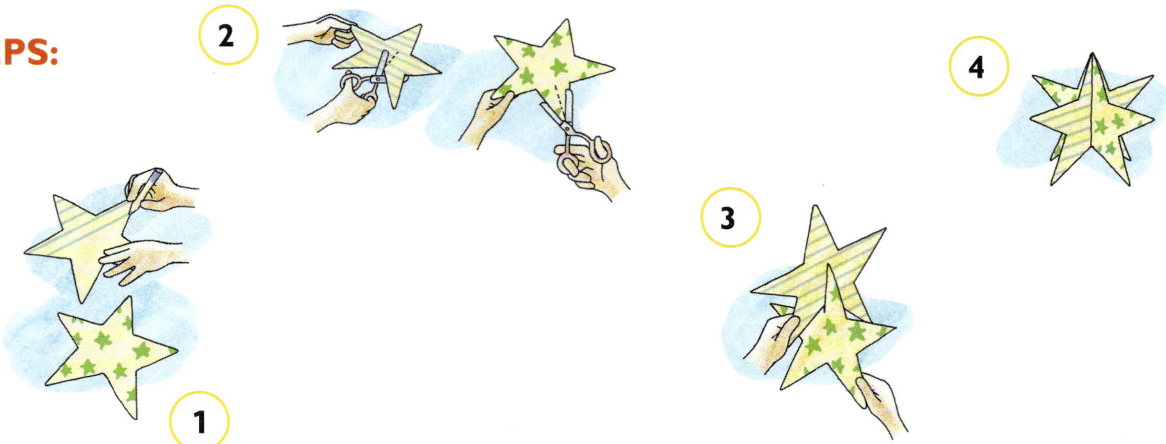

A Photo Frame (1)

YOU NEED:

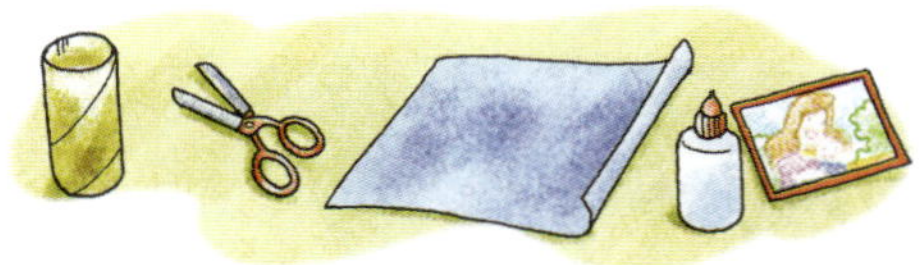

STEPS:

1

2

3

4

A Photo Frame (2)

YOU NEED:

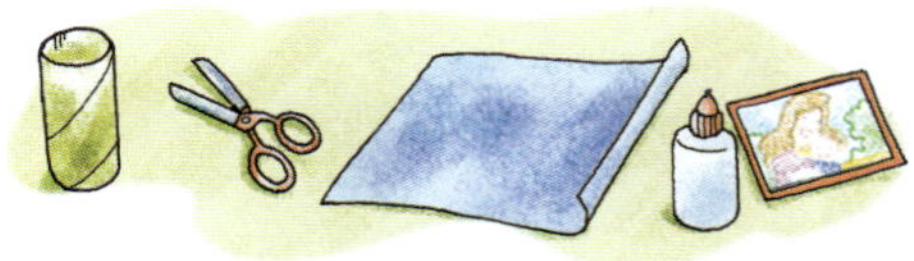

STEPS:

A Coat-Hanger Mobile

YOU NEED:

STEPS:

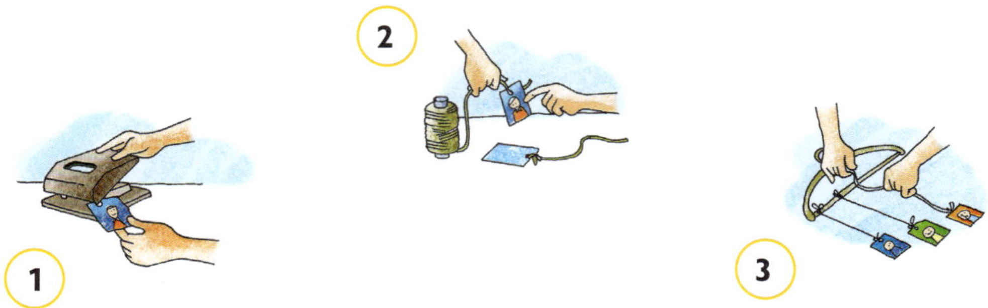

MACMILLAN

Editora: Wilma Moura
Editora assistente: Ana Paula Landi
Assistente editorial: Glauce Perusso Pereira Dias Muniz

Edição de arte, projeto gráfico, capa, editoração eletrônica: AMj Studio
Ilustrações: Gaiola Estúdio, Paulo Borges (Projects) e Amilton Ishikawa/AMj Studio
Fotos: Fabio Colombini (págs. 56 e 63 - hamster e tartaruga); demais fotos: © 2008 Jupiterimages Corporation

Dados Internacionais de Catalogação na Publicação (CIP)
(Câmara Brasileira do Livro, SP, Brasil)

Rodovalho, Ana Cláudia
Spaghetti kids : 2° ano / Ana Cláudia Rodovalho, Karina Torres F. Silva, Luciana Renda B. Melo. -- 4. ed. atual. -- São Paulo : Macmillan, 2008.

ISBN 978-85-7418-644-3 (student's book)
ISBN 978-85-7418-639-9 (teacher's book)

1. Inglês (Ensino fundamental) I. Silva, Karina Torres F. II. Melo, Luciana Renda B. III. Título.

08-02380 CDD-372.652

Índices para catálogo sistemático:
1. Inglês : Ensino fundamental 372.652

4ª edição - 2008
Macmillan do Brasil
Rua José Felix de Oliveira, 383 – Granja Viana – 06708-645 – Cotia – São Paulo – Brasil
Atendimento ao professor: São Paulo – Capital – (0XX11) 4613 2278
Demais localidades: 0800 168877 – Fax: (0XX11) 4612 6098
E-mail: elt@macmillan.com.br - Website: www.macmillan.com.br

impresso no Brasil - Ricargraf - fev/2018

STICKERS

PÁG. 11

GOOD MORNING

GOOD AFTERNOON

GOOD NIGHT

GOODBYE

PÁG. 11

PÁG. 19

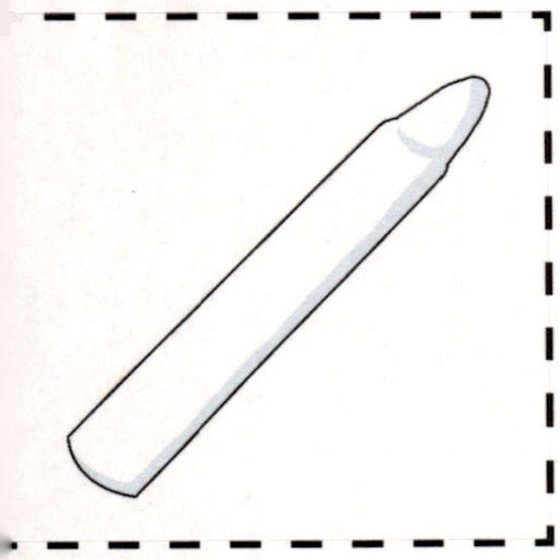

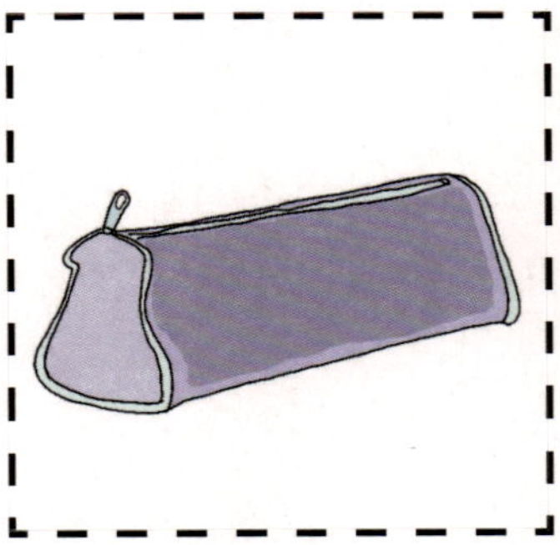

PÁG. 24

PERMANEN

STICKERS

PÁG. 35

PÁG. 57

PÁG. 67

PÁG. 77

PÁG. 93

STICKERS - MY WORD BOOK

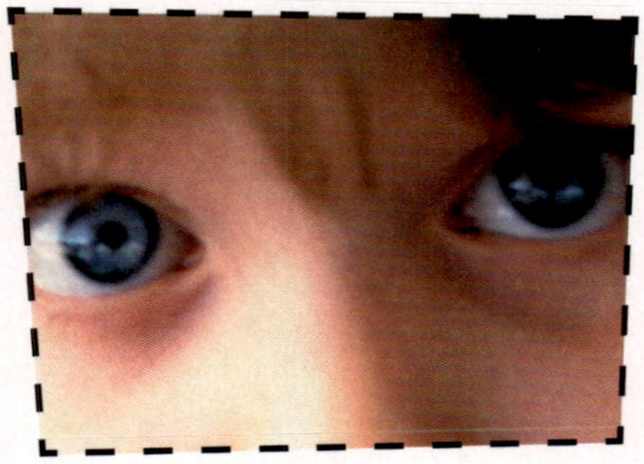

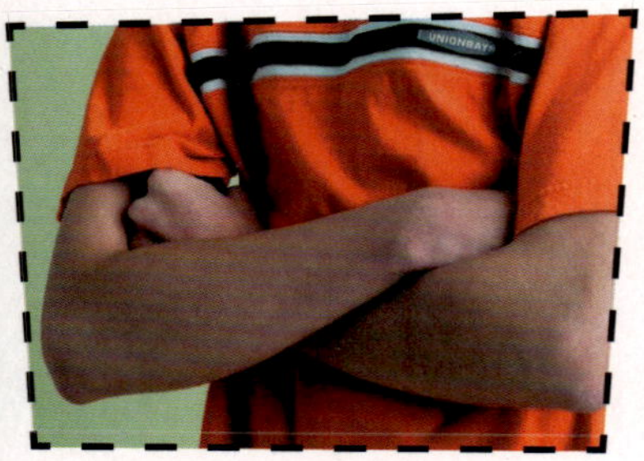

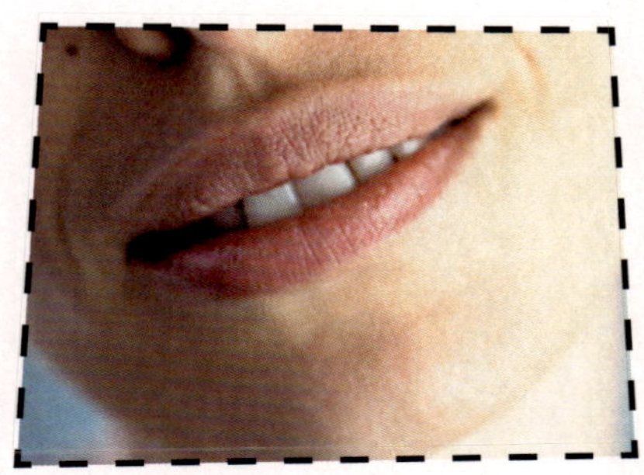

STICKERS - MY WORD BOOK

STICKERS - MY WORD BOOK

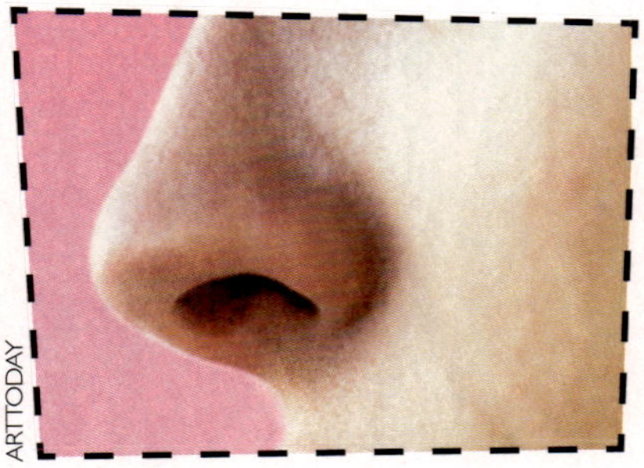

ARTTODAY

ARTTODAY

ARTTODAY